Fab Girls™ Guide to

Friendship Hardship

By Phoebe Kitanidis

Discovery Girls, Inc.

CALIFORNIA

Discovery Girls, Inc.
4300 Stevens Creek Blvd., Suite 190
San Jose, California 95129

Book design by Asha Hossain and Alex Saymo.

ISBN 978-1-934766-00-2

Visit Discovery Girls' web site at www.discoverygirls.com.

Printed in the United States of America.

Dedication

Dedicated to the thousands of girls who have taken the time to write to Discovery Girls magazine to share your ideas, thoughts, personal stories, and yes, even your problems. All of us who work at Discovery Girls, Inc. have been deeply touched by your letters. You are a constant source of insight and inspiration, and the reason we have created this book.

Acknowledgments

I'd like to send a special thank you to all the girls who have read Discovery Girls magazine over the years and have generously shared your thoughts, ideas, and experiences with us. Without you, there would be no Discovery Girls magazine and definitely no Discovery Girls books. I feel so very fortunate to have had the opportunity to work with my dedicated and talented staff: Julia Clause, Ashley DeGree, Naomi Kirsten, Katherine Inouye Lau, Alex Saymo, Bill Tsukuda, Sarah Verney, and interns Lyn Meheula, Laura Riparbelli, and Nick Tran. Your enthusiasm and ability to keep your sense of humor while meeting insane deadlines, your willingness to work long hours, your amazing creative energy, and your insistence on always striving to get better and better have meant more to me than you will ever know—my deepest appreciation! Also, a very special thank you to artists Kathleen Uno, Bill Tsukuda, and Rhiannon Cunag for helping bring the Fab Girls to life.

Catherine Lee
PUBLISHER
DISCOVERY GIRLS

Meet the Fab Girls

Carmen

Dallas

Hi! We're Carmen and Dallas Fabrulézziano, but you can call us the Fab Girls! Why "*Fab*"? Well, we came up with that because Fabrulézziano isn't exactly the easiest name to say, and besides, we're totally *fabulous*! Ha, ha—just kidding.

We may be twins, but we're *totally* different. Carmen plans everything down to the smallest detail—from her glamorous outfits to her perfectly edited homework. She **can't live without her personal organizer**—it even helps her remember the birthdays of practically everyone in the eighth grade! Dallas, on the other hand, is too busy coming up with amazing ideas to organize anything. She's **super smart and super creative,** and you can always count on her to tell you the truth—no matter what! But even though we are so different, **we still make a great team.**

No one ever has a tough time telling us apart, and that's what's so absolutely awesome about being a Fab Girl! Even though **we're complete opposites,** we still share that special sisterly bond that makes us **the best of friends**...well, most of the time!

So, what exactly are we doing here? Discovery Girls asked us to help you through these **crazy, confusing middle-school years.** And who better to go through them with than a couple of fun Fab Girls who know exactly how you feel? We'll give it to you straight and tell you **everything you need to know about friendship.** And remember: With the Fab Girls around, **you're never alone!**

xoxo

carmen
& Dallas

Name: Carmen

Hobbies: Acting, reading romance novels, and perfecting my chocolate-chip cookie recipe.

My biggest dream: To win an Academy Award.

I never leave home without: My planner! It's a minute-by-minute outline of my busy days—dance lessons, friends' birthdays, homework, auditions...I'd be lost without it!

Everyone knows: I'll be totally famous one day! I mean, I already had a small part in a movie...

No one knows: I'm actually very shy. When I have to give a presentation in class, I get totally nauseous.

Biggest pet peeve: People who don't RSVP. I'd love to give half my school a crash course in etiquette!

My take on Dallas: She always knows when I'm feeling down, even if I haven't said a word. She helps me think about things in completely different ways, and I'm my old self in no time!

Name: Dallas

Hobbies: Running track, photography, and playing the drums in my band. (I'm the only girl!)

My biggest dream: Yearbook editor today, world-traveling Pulitzer Prize-winning photojournalist tomorrow!

I never leave home without: Painting a tiny star under my right eye...it's my trademark!

Everyone knows: I'm a math wiz. As math team captain, I totally convinced the principal that we deserve jackets this year.

No one knows: I have a crush on the lead guitarist in my band. (But—SHHH! Don't tell!)

Biggest pet peeve: Girls who gossip and judge others. Don't get me started!

My take on Carmen: She's the most thoughtful sister! Every year on our birthday she creates a new scrapbook for me with highlights of my entire year... with doodles and pictures to match.

Contents

Welcome to Middle-School Friendships

Remember when making friends was as simple as passing the girl next to you a red crayon? Back in kindergarten, you could set your snack down next to a stranger and— by the end of recess—be giggling and having the time of your life with a new *friend*.

Flash forward to the start of middle school. **Suddenly fashion matters, rumors fly, and kids break off into cliques.** How are you supposed to find true friends and a place to belong? How can you *be* a good friend? Should you join a clique? And how do you avoid getting your self-esteem crushed by mean girls and frenemies along the way?

We wrote this book after reading thousands of letters from girls who read *Discovery Girls* magazine. **We get tons of reader mail about our friendship articles,** and Ali, our advice columnist, gets so many letters about friendship problems, cliques, and popularity she can't possibly answer even a fraction of them. All of this made us realize just how complicated and confusing friendship can be in middle-school. For example: What exactly *are* you supposed to do when a mean girl cuts you down in front of all your friends? And how should you handle it when a friend accuses *you* of being mean and hurting her feelings? Worst of all, what do you do when the girls you consider your very best friends don't seem to share your point of view...at least, not anymore? If you're feeling anxious about questions like these, or about cliques, confidence, popularity, or the real reasons girls act mean, **you're not alone.**

In these pages, we'll show you how to tell the difference between good and bad friends *before* you hand over your feelings (and your secrets) to them. Then we'll teach you how to be the best friend you can be, how to meet new people, how to find the friendships you deserve and be truly popular...as well as how to save a friendship where one or both of you have made a few mistakes. Whether you're battling a girl bully, stuck in a fading friendship, or caught in the "wanna-be-popular" trap, **we'll break down the solutions for you step by step.**

True friendship is a gift. It brings you sympathy, support, and sheer fun. And as middle school stresses pile on, you *need* strong friendships. **Now is the time to get clear on how you deserve to be treated by others (hint: with respect).** To free your life of poisonous friendships forever, making room for true-blue friends who respect and understand you, who run up and give you a hug when you've had a rough day, and who keep you up past midnight on Friday nights, talking and laughing and having the time of your lives. That's the kind of first-rate friendship you deserve, so from now on, accept no substitutes!

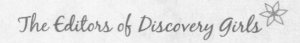

The Editors of Discovery Girls

Chapter One

How Do Your Friendships Rate?

"My best friend is the one who brings out the best in me."
–Henry Ford

Take an Honest Look at Your Friendships

Are you ready to take a totally honest look at what's happening in your friendships? This quiz is a great place to start. As you answer each question, think about your best friend...then take it again on the friendships that cause the most drama in your life, or any friendship you think needs help!

??QUIZ?? Good Friendship...or Bad?

1. You're trying on clothes together at the mall when you squeeze into a pair of jeans that just don't look good on your body. Your friend:

a. Takes that moment to mention that her cousin just lost five pounds on a low-carb diet. "Hey, you should e-mail her and ask for some tips!"

b. Instantly reminds you of how great you looked in the miniskirt you tried on earlier.

c. Doesn't even notice what you're wearing—she's too busy putting together an outfit for herself.

2. Star-crossed schedules: You and your BFF have zero classes together all semester. How she handles it:

a. Meets cool new people in her classes and introduces them to you at lunch.

b. Meets cool new people in her classes and starts ditching you at lunch.

c. Cries, floods your locker with anxious notes, and glues herself to your side every non-class moment, complaining about the "tragedy" of not getting to be in class with you.

3. The yearbook has you as the "Class Bookworm," but lately you've been itching to try out a very un-bookish activity: skateboarding! When you show your friend your cool new board, she says (after picking up her jaw):

a. "Ha, ha, you, a skater chick? Sure you wouldn't rather read a book about it?"

b. "Wow, that doesn't sound like you at all. But, okay, if it's what you want."

c. "That's so great that you're brave enough to try something different. You'll be doing ollies in no time!"

4. Overnight, your friend has become a boy magnet. After three boys ask her to the fall dance, you confess to feeling the teeniest bit jealous, to which she responds:

more on next page!

a. "You're jealous? Well, gosh, what am I supposed to do? It's not my fault they all like me!"
b. "Don't worry, I get jealous of you sometimes, too. Especially during the soccer season, 'cause you're such a star!"
c. "Hey, just remember, being pretty isn't everything. You have tons of other great qualities!"

5. Before your friend passes her brand-new digital camera into your eager hands, she spends *lots* of time going over:

a. The camera's many cool features, so you can try 'em all.
b. How expensive the camera would be to replace if, say, it got broken.
c. The camera's quick-erase feature since, "You take really bad pictures, no offense!"

6. When she asks to borrow your favorite book, you:

a. Buy your BFF her own copy instead. You don't want to get into another fight about her not returning your stuff.
b. Eagerly hand over the whole series—you can't wait to talk about the characters together when she's done!
c. Remind her not to scrawl her crush's name all over the margins like she did with the last book you loaned her.

7. The darkest day of your friendship was when she:

a. Snapped at you for no reason (and apologized later).
b. Got mad and threatened to tell everyone your secrets.
c. Tearfully announced that her family might be moving to another state!

Give yourself the following points for each of your answers, then add them up to find your score:

SCORING
1) a. 1 b. 3 c. 2   5) a. 3 b. 2 c. 1
2) a. 3 b. 1 c. 2   6) a. 1 b. 3 c. 2
3) a. 1 b. 2 c. 3   7) a. 2 b. 1 c. 3
4) a. 2 b. 3 c. 1

7–12 Points Poisonous Patti

Let's see, she's mean, she's untrustworthy, she may actually be trying to make you feel bad....Nope, it's not your imagination: This girl is not your friend—she's a frenemy wearing your BFF necklace! You deserve better, and deep down you know it. Let go of her and make room for some real friendships. P.S. You may need some help learning to seek out truly supportive pals who appreciate you for who you are, but don't worry...help is only a page away! Keep reading...

13–18 Points Average Annie

She's a good, solid pal who's fun to hang with and always there when you need her. Sure, you're not as close as you could be, but oh well, what can you do? Actually...there's a lot you can do. You can take simple steps right now that will perk up not only this friendship but all your friendships, taking them to a higher level of trust, caring, and respect, and yes, fun...we'll show you how!

19–21 Points True-Blue Tabitha

Whatever you do, don't let go of this girl! She's supportive, thoughtful, honest, and caring. She knows what "friendship" means and she's willing to pour energy into yours to keep it shiny. But though this friendship's golden, you don't want to depend on just one pal in middle school. Besides, you're bound to run into people who aren't as easy to get along with as she is. Read on, and we'll show you how to add 10 essential new friendships to your life, how to avoid drama, and how to make all your friendships as terrific as this one!

Wait...My Friendship Isn't So Bad!

Maybe you're thinking, "Hey, no fair! My friendship scored low, but that's because this quiz only focuses on the bad stuff that happens! What about all the fun we had Friday, giggling hysterically till two a.m.? What about the way she French braids my hair, or the hours she spent helping me with my science project? Our friendship isn't all bad!"

You're right, it's not. No friendship is all drama and misery. If she was mean to you 100 percent of the time, you'd simply walk away. But each friendship is made up of thousands of small moments, and some of those moments can be fabulous even if most of the friendship is, well...*not*. On the other hand, there's no such thing as a *perfect* friendship, either. Even the best friendship can have its shaky moments. No wonder it's easy to get confused about which ones are worth saving!

So how do you figure it all out? If you came up with "Poisonous Patti" on the quiz, that's a red flag something is seriously wrong. But if your friend is an "Average Annie" or if you're just not convinced that it's that bad, try looking at how you feel *most of the time* you're with her.

In a true friendship, you generally feel relaxed and confident. You know you can be yourself. You're comfortable, not terrified you'll say the wrong thing. And when you're together, you don't always have to do what *she* wants; *your* thoughts and needs count just as much as hers. You don't even have to hide embarrassing things about yourself, because the two of you can just laugh about them. And no matter how tough a challenge you're facing in life, a good friendship brings you comfort and confidence, because you know your friend is standing by you.

A good friendship is like a secret superpower you can call on anytime.

A bad friendship, on the other hand, often feels like a roller coaster.
When she's being nice, you have a blast together...but you're still on edge, nervous and stressed, waiting for the next sharp drop. Your stomach lurches every time you unfold her latest note: Will this one be friendly...or peppered with her snarky little put-downs? You beam with relief when you see her approaching your lunch table—see, she *didn't* ditch you; she *is* your BFF...at least for today.

a bad friendship steals your self-confidence and stresses you out.

It's hard to be at your best in a friendship like this! You end up confused and angry at the way she treats you, but you're afraid of losing her friendship, so you put up with the disrespect. Deep inside, resentment starts building, until soon you're thinking some pretty nasty thoughts behind that friendly smile—and about your own best friend! You find yourself acting extra-competitive when the two of you play one-on-one b-ball. You're secretly thrilled when her crush doesn't like her back. But then you feel guilty... and mad at yourself, too, for letting her trample your feelings time and again.

Does any of this sound familiar? If so, it may be time to decide this friendship just isn't what you're looking for. But before you make up your mind to end it, remember...the key is to look at how things go *most of the time*. Remember, no friendship is perfect. Even true-blue pals can accidentally hurt your feelings or say things they later regret. Let's say you snag the lead role in a play you both tried out for, and she doesn't seem happy for you...in fact, she's acting snippy and jealous! Does this mean she's a bad friend? Not necessarily—after all, she's human, and she wanted that part as much as you did. Your friend is bound to suffer a few bad moods and moments of insecurity (just like you!).

So if most of the time, you feel your friend brings out the very best in you, you've got a friendship worth keeping, and you should do everything in your power to be the friend she deserves in return. But if this friendship tears down your self-confidence and leaves you feeling angry and confused...well, you can do better. You deserve real, true-blue friendships, and we'll show you how to get them.

> "My friend Lena is an amazing modern dancer, while ice-skating and art are my things. We cheer for each other and if one of us gets an award or recognition, you'd think we both earned it!"
>
> —Geron, age 10, Pa.

How Does Your Friendship Measure Up?

✔ Check off the statements below that truly describe how you feel about your friendship. If you check off six or more, your friendship is golden...two or less, this friendship needs work!

☑ When something good happens to one of you, you're both jumping up and down with excitement—it's as if it happened to both of you!

☑ After a whole day of hanging out with her, you feel happy to be you.

☑ You can relax and be yourself around her...you can even make dumb jokes or wear silly pajamas if you feel like it.

☑ When someone tries to put you down or exclude you, she's the first person to step up in your defense.

☑ She notices nice things about you and brightens your day with little comments like, "Your hair looks really good today!" or "Nice job on the math homework!"

☑ She accepts your taste in clothes, music, books, and hairstyles, even if it doesn't quite match her own.

☑ She listens when you have something to tell her and makes it clear that she cares about how you feel.

☑ When it comes to friendly favors like loaning lunch money or helping with homework, her generosity matches yours.

☑ Neither one of you plays the sidekick to the other's star—you're both stars!

☑ If you were ever in serious trouble, you'd want her to know so she could help you.

Chapter Two

Mean Girls and Frenemies

"False friends are worse than open enemies."
—Scottish Proverb

Eight Frenemy Behaviors

While you can't always predict if someone will be a good friend, you can sometimes tell that they'll be a bad friend. Bad friends all have some pattern of mean or unfair behavior they persist in, even when you tell them they're hurting your feelings! Fortunately, if you know what to look for, you can spot these poisonous behaviors early on, before you get too close. To help you, we've put together a glossary of bad-friend patterns to watch out for.

> Bad friends do the same mean things over and over.

Keep in mind, though, that we're focusing on only one aspect of a girl's behavior. In real life, people are way more complicated than a one-note description. So even if you meet someone who seems to fit one of these stereotypes to a tee, remind yourself that she's a real person like you, not a cartoon, and there's probably a lot you don't know about her. Still, if you recognize a pattern to her behavior that matches any of these descriptions…proceed with caution!

The User

She borrows your favorite sweater and brings it back with a huge tomato sauce stain. Loan her five bucks and that's money you'll never see again. In a healthy friendship, sharing goes both ways, but somewhere down the line, The User got the (wrong) idea that she deserves special treatment from others. She'll run you ragged doing her favors, but if *you* ever dare to ask *her* for anything, she'll kick up a fuss…and weasel out of it!

The Gossip

She always knows who got detention for back-talking the science teacher. She knows who every girl has a crush on, and whether it's returned. Yet no matter how many times you've caught her spreading rumors, part of you still wants to trust this girl. Why? Because gossips are often friendly, likeable, outgoing people. Unfortunately, they also trade your secrets for attention. Having an audience is so much fun, they'll keep talking till they've said it all. Until The Gossip learns to button her lip, don't tell her anything private!

The Part-Time Bully

Yikes, the girl's got a split personality…part friendly, part scary! Her temper can turn on a dime, and when she's not in one of her nicer moods, she'll go so far as to sneer in your face, scream insults, threaten you, and even shove you or hit you. Her softer moments may fool you into thinking she's changed, but the "changes" never last long. Whatever is making this girl angry has nothing to do with you. You can't fix her problems...and you don't have to put up with her mean moods. Instead of getting upset next time she growls at you, simply walk away. And if you feel at all threatened, *don't* hesitate to bring in an adult!

The Cling-On

She follows you around like a helpless puppy. Invites herself over to your house every day and won't take a hint when it's *time to go home*. Sadly, The Cling-On is too desperate for your friendship to notice you're not having fun with her. Be honest, did you actually *want* to be friends, or did she just guilt you into hanging out because you felt sorry for her? Maybe The Cling-On isn't exactly mean, but she's still poisonous in that she'll keep you from having healthy friendships with other people. (Note: not to be confused with the slightly jealous best friend, who may have a hard time dealing with the fact that you have other friends, but who *isn't* totally dependent on you.)

The Snob

Whether she's bragging about a dream vacation or curling her lip at someone's non-designer shoes, The Snob tries to convince you that she's better than you...because her stuff is better than your stuff. And all too often it works. Even when it goes against everything you believe, it's hard not to end up feeling envious when The Snob's around. But look carefully: Underneath it all, this girl is terrified that without her cool stuff, she'd be nothing. If you know a snob who's otherwise a nice person, make sure she knows you like her for who she is, not for what she has… she just might get the message and come down to Earth!

I know a girl who sounds just like "The Snob!" It's hard to believe she's just insecure, but I guess it does make sense. Why else would she need to impress people with all her great stuff?

The Drama Queen

She pages you 911 in the middle of your favorite show. Gabs your ear off in class… when you're reviewing for a big test. Whether it's family issues or boy trouble, The Drama Queen is *always* in the middle of a crisis…and soon you will be too, when she pulls you in! Sure, it can feel exciting to act as advisor to this larger-than-life diva, but real friends deserve *equal* time onstage.

I've definitely been called "dramatic," but I'd never be a drama queen in a friendship! I want my friend to feel like a star, too!

The Kidder ✓

The nerve! This frenemy makes fun of you in front of your other buds, then adds the magic words, "Just kidding!" so you can't be mad at her. What is her problem? In *her* mind at least, it's you: Odds are, she's jealous of you big time. That's why she's focusing so much attention on putting you down even while she tries to be close to you as a friend. The Kidder would love to take your confidence down a notch or two, but she doesn't want to risk losing your friendship...so she hides behind mean humor instead.

The Backstabber

She's a pro at *starting* friendships. For a while, The Backstabber can morph herself into exactly the kind of friend you're looking for. In fact, she may even seem like a *perfect friend.* But just about the time you really get attached, she finds some dramatic way to dump you for her *next* BFF. Maybe one day she'll learn how to have lasting friendships, but it's not going to happen tomorrow, or even this year (sorry!). So if you see someone end a ton of friendships fast—and with tons of drama—think twice before you get close!

Poisonous Friend...or Friend Who Made a Mistake?

We wouldn't be too surprised if you felt a little worried at this point. After all that talk about poisonous friends, you may have a sinking feeling that one or two of those descriptions had a passing

resemblance to someone you see in the mirror. Don't panic…
because the truth is, every single one of us has been rude, mean, or
disrespectful to a friend at some point!

**So, if everyone makes mistakes, how can you tell the difference between
poisonous friends and keepers?** Here's the key: A true friend won't
keep doing something that makes you feel bad. If you tell her she
hurt your feelings, she won't brush you off—she'll try her very best
to make it up to you and avoid making the same mistake again.
Bottom line: She'll honestly care how you feel.

Why Do They Do It?

**Though they show it in different ways (gossiping, bullying, hogging the
limelight),** the same thing drives some girls to treat people badly.
What is it? In a word, they're *unhappy*. Something inside them is
bothering them in a big, bad way…and stopping them from having
real, loving, give-and-take friendships.

> "I've had friends who turned out to be
> two-faced or liars. My mom says I'm
> very lucky because I have something
> special that they don't. I'm happy with
> who I am. That means I don't have to
> lie or be fake with my friends."
>
> —Orlina, age 12, Calif.

"Yeah, right!" you may be thinking. "The meanest girl I know doesn't seem unhappy at all. She has tons of friends and she struts around school like she's 10 feet tall. Her self-esteem must be through the roof!" Are you absolutely sure of that? Here's a simple way to test our theory that peaceful, contented people who love their lives do *not* act like jerks.

First, imagine you're in a fantastic mood. It's your birthday, and you just beat your record for swimming the backstroke, your crush told you he thinks you're the coolest girl in school, and you just earned a big, beautiful A+ in geometry, your hardest class. You're on top of the world when your best friend walks into the room sporting a dramatic new 'do.

What would you do?
(Pick "a" or "b.")

a. Give her a big smile and say, "Wow, cool haircut!"
b. Turn to the popular acquaintance sitting next to you and whisper, "Omigosh, she looks like an ugly boy with that hair!"

 See how easy that choice was?

Now let's turn it around. Pretend you're having an absolutely rotten day. You *flunked* the geometry test this time, while your friend got the A+. Your dad yelled at you for nothing, your parents aren't going to be able to pay for swim team this year, and the most popular boy in school pointed and laughed when you dropped your burrito on the floor at lunch. *Now* when you see your best friend sail into the room with her daring new haircut, isn't there a teeny part of you that's tempted to make a funny (if slightly cruel) comment about her to someone? Still no?

Okay. Now imagine if you felt that awful day after day…week after week. You feel empty and alone, like no one on Earth really knows the real you. You look in the mirror and hate what you see. You feel like people only pretend to like you. You don't trust anyone; they're only going to turn on you like everyone does. Do you feel your inner mean girl coming out by imagining yourself so unhappy? If not, you're a very strong girl indeed!

So how did your poisonous friend become unhappy in the first place? In a way, it doesn't matter…because whatever her problems are, they don't give her the right to mistreat you. For example, maybe your pal who acts like The Kidder is dealing with a difficult situation at home that's left her feeling like she's not worth much. Maybe your next-door neighbor who acts like The Part-Time Bully is constantly picked on

I hate to admit it, but I might act mean if I were that unhappy. It's really hard to be nice all the time when you're so upset inside.

by an older sibling. But while your friend may have reasons for behaving the way she does, reasons are not the same thing as excuses. And although you may be a helpful person who likes to fix things, it's not your job to fix *her*. If you stick around and try, she'll keep on treating you badly till you're feeling just as miserable as she is. Walk away instead, but try not to walk away angry. As much as she's hurt you, she's just a kid like you and she's unhappy right now.

When you think about it, in a lot of ways you're actually <u>luckier</u> than she is!

Dealing With Mean Girls

Even if you steer clear of poisonous friendships, you're still bound to have run-ins with meanies at school, girls who aren't claiming to be your BFF. So, how do you prevent mean classmates from spoiling your mood, tarnishing your rep, and eating away at your self-respect?

1. Understand that it's not about you.

Here's an example of a nasty encounter that could ruin your morning... or not, depending on how you "read" it. You're striding down the hall, feeling like a million bucks in your cute new outfit, when suddenly you bump into a popular girl. She sticks her hands on her hips and says, "Ohmigosh, white jeans are *so* not cool anymore!" You freeze and stammer, but she's already walked on. Sure, deep down you know you shouldn't take her comment to heart. But that's easier said than done, especially when it was delivered by a popular girl, someone everybody listens to. If she says your jeans are out of style, why *shouldn't* you listen? It must be true...she said it...she must be right. Your confidence is history.

But what *really* happened here? On the surface, it looks like she put you in your place by stating an unfortunate truth. You made an embarrassing fashion mistake, and should feel uncool. But remember how feeling unhappy made you more likely to say or do something mean? It's the same for everyone. When a mean girl picks on you, it almost always is about something being wrong with *her*.

Like what? Well, maybe she's upset about something else entirely, and taking it out on you. Maybe that popular girl's older sister cut *her* down at breakfast. Maybe her best friend is moving away and she's mad at the world. It could also be that she's rude just because she *can* be. Some people do feel a surge of power from being mean to those they consider less cool than themselves. In other words, maybe the girl who insulted you is simply a bit of a bully.

Here's another possibility: It could just be she's the type of person who blurts out rude comments without thinking. She might be shocked—even confused—to hear you were upset by her comment. From her perspective, she was just voicing whatever thoughts came into her head...and she's already forgotten about it!

Of course, you'll never know for sure why she chose to pick on you. But when you think about it, any of the above explanations seems more plausible than, "My jeans are out of style and somehow I didn't know, my mom didn't know, the people in the store and the designers didn't know, and only this one mean girl at school happened to know." Notice how all those other explanations have nothing to do with you at all, and everything to do with her personality and her problems. Your clothes remain as cool as they were a few minutes ago. And your mood can and *should* stay cool, too!

When a mean girl picks on you, it is almost always about something being wrong with <u>her</u>.

2. Pick Your Battles

Most slights are so unimportant that the smartest thing is to just ignore them. Ask yourself: What's at stake here? Is the person who's being mean to you important in your life? Will there be any long-term fallout from her disrespecting you? Your answers will tell you if the fight's worth winning. If you're racing the bell to French class and two random eighth graders snicker and point as you dash by, it's clearly not worth stopping to ask them what their problem is. Instead, take a deep breath and remind yourself that you can choose to shrug it off. The only way to win a fight like this is *not* to have it.

But what if your rep among your buddies is at stake? For example, you're chatting with a group of girls when one of them reaches out to touch your shirt. "*Ew*, I can't believe you wore that!" she says, giggling. "Did you, like, find it in the dumpster?" Now everybody's looking at you. If you walk away, they'll assume you couldn't handle it—that you're easily upset and intimidated. On the other hand, if you just stand there like a statue, they'll notice that you let people get away with pushing you around. It'll be open season on teasing you until you finally *do* take a stand. So, what should you do?

 Switch gears.

Instead of your usual "walk away" approach, this situation calls for you to be assertive and relaxed. *Assertive* in that you're not going to let anybody walk all over you. You're not too timid and scared to look her in the eye and respond. *Relaxed* because you're also not going to get upset and overreact, either.

What to say? Instead of hitting the other girl with a Mack truck of anger in response, try some humor. For example, you might agree with her. "Yeah, the dumpster had a great sale on Saturday. I got my skirt there, too!" Another pretty safe response is to pretend you've received a wonderful compliment. "Oh, thank you very much! You always say the nicest things!" You can play it straight or ham it up as you thank them for the lovely words of praise. Humor can break up the tension in the conversation, making people feel better again.

Are you surprised we didn't suggest confronting her with a heartfelt complaint like, "That wasn't very nice, and I'd appreciate it if you wouldn't talk about my clothes like that anymore"? Actually, there's nothing wrong with expressing that thought *later*—especially if the person is your friend and she keeps talking to you in a way you don't appreciate. But if you say it now, in front of an audience and in the heat of the moment, it could all too easily spiral into a big fight. If you still want to confront her later, it's much better to talk one-on-one.

Beyond Slights and Put-Downs

They're relatively rare, but some mean-girl encounters are too risky to ignore and too heavy to fix with a joke. Let's say you're being harassed by a girl who's decided to make your life miserable. She sends you nasty IM-s, tries to turn your friends against you, tells random boys that you want to go out with

Make sure your friends know what's going on, too—especially if your "enemy" is trying to involve them.

them—anything to upset you and make you feel bad. This is no joke! If her behavior is seriously affecting your friendships, your confidence, even your schoolwork, it's time to call in your support system. Tell your parents what's going on. Together you can go to a trusted authority, like the school counselor, for help. This bully needs to get a strong, clear message that what she's doing is unacceptable.

??QUIZ?? Are You Mean?

You still remember every time a "mean girl" made you feel bad, but has the shoe ever been on the other foot? How often have you hurt someone? Take this quiz to see if you're really as nice as you want to be.

In the past year, have you:

1. Blabbed a friend's juicy secret?

a. When it comes to my friends' secrets, I'm like a locked safe.
b. I spilled the beans once…and I still regret it!
c. Sure, but I always tell the other person not to tell anyone, so it's not that bad.

2. Complained about one friend to another behind the first friend's back (instead of talking to her directly).

a. Only if the two friends have never met.
b. Sometimes if I'm feeling really frustrated...even though I know it can cause extra drama.
c. Yep—nothing wrong with a little healthy venting!

3. Cracked a joke or been sarcastic about another person's outfit? (Example: "Whoa, nice pants...if this were the 70s!")

a. No way—insulting other people's style isn't my style.
b. Okay, so I try not to be the fashion police, but sometimes a few snarky comments do slip out.
c. Hey, when someone goes around dressed like a total weirdo, they're begging for it.

4. Made fun of others behind their backs for something that was not their fault (like their height, weight, hair color, or accent)?

a. No matter how I felt about someone, I can't imagine being so cruel that I'd make fun of them for stuff they can't help!
b. Eh, I've done it...but then I didn't feel so great about myself.
c. Yeah, but it's harmless—it's not like they're ever going to find out!

5. Continued to tease someone who was showing signs of getting seriously upset?

a. I don't tease people unless I know them well...otherwise it's easy to go too far.
b. Yes...I should have backed off sooner.
c. Yes...but they were being way oversensitive.

6. Gotten snippy with a friend because you were tired, jealous, or angry for some other unrelated reason?

a. Being upset doesn't give me a free pass to be nasty, so no.
b. Once or twice, and I apologized afterward. (I really was sorry, too!)
c. Doesn't everyone? I'm sure my friends don't take my bad moods personally.

7. Pushed a pal into doing something she wasn't sure she wanted to do (taking a dare, asking a boy out)?

a. Nope—I might suggest something, but I wouldn't pressure her if she said no.
b. Now that I think about it, a group of us did kind of pressure our friend to do something. Hmm. That wasn't cool.
c. It's not my fault. I didn't physically force her to do anything.

Add 'em up! ✓

Mostly A's
Mean Ain't Your Scene

Congratulations! You're almost never mean, because you make a point of treating everyone with kindness and respect—whether they happen to be in the room with you or not. You're wise enough to know what a difference being nice makes to the people in your life. As a bonus, you enjoy peace of mind because you don't have to feel guilty or make excuses for hurting people's feelings all the time. Just keep doing what you're doing, girl—your kindness makes the world a better place.

Mostly B's
Don't Mean to Be Mean

✓

Congratulations! You've made your share of mistakes in friendships, but we still think you're doing great. Why? Because you're able to see your past errors and, hopefully, learn from them. It's not easy to admit you've messed up, but that's what you do if you're a kind, caring person striving to be a better friend. Just be careful that you don't repeat old mistakes...and start paying more attention to being considerate from now on. You'll get there!

Mostly C's
Mean Machine

Uh-oh…is it time to slap a skull-and-crossbones sticker on your forehead? You act mean way too often, and you're even quick to justify your actions. So what's up? Could it be that you think being mean makes you seem cool and tough? Or is your meanness a shield to stop other people from being mean to you? Whatever your reasons, it's time to change. Otherwise, you're setting yourself up for a rude awakening when your friends finally get tired of your nastiness—and they will!

Chapter Three

To Clique or Not to Clique

"Surround yourself only with people who are going to lift you higher."

–Oprah Winfrey

What's Up With All the Cliques?

So far, we've mostly been discussing one-on-one friendships. But maybe you've noticed that once you hit middle school, everyone seems to travel in packs. Back in elementary school, BFF meant two-by-two, but lately everyone's rushing to get accepted into the coolest clique they possibly can.

" My friends are like a little family. We get together for movies every Friday night and make chocolate popcorn. We think it's delicious but everyone else thinks it's gross. None of us have boyfriends yet, but we all think the same actors are cute."

—Jeanne, age 12, Wash.

For many girls, cliques have a bad name. After all, when the wrong combination of personalities gets together, something pretty scary can happen. Some girls start telling their "friends" what to do, right down to what to wear and whom to talk to. Other girls follow along because it's easier than standing up to their bossy friends. Girls who *do* stand up for themselves may get made fun of or gossiped about, or even kicked out of the group. Fights break out. Feelings get hurt. Before you know it, all the clique members are sitting in the school counselor's office, crying and looking sorry.

Thank goodness, though, not *every* group is like that. In fact, if you drop a few girls with similar interests into one classroom—or street, or camp, or ballet school—something magical often happens. They hang. They bond. They come up with wacky inside jokes that no one else on the planet understands. Soon they've got their very own customs and routines. They cheer for each other's successes and support each other through challenging moments. Before you know it, everyone sees them as a group. And it all feels so effortless, so natural.

No wonder some girls desperately want to be part of a clique. If your BFF is home sick with the flu on the day you get a D on a quiz, find out your crush has a new girlfriend, *and* get picked on by the class bully, you've got all those other shoulders to cry on. It's like having your own personal support group. And in the large, often impersonal world of middle school, a group that welcomes you and lets you know you belong can feel like an oasis in the desert.

When you're surrounded by friends, there's always someone there for you.

Even in a healthy clique, though, there can be a price to be paid for belonging. When you're hanging with your group, you're far less likely to notice other people around you, so you may be missing out on some pretty cool friendships. If you're feeling shy and scared, your group gives you a safe place to hide...but that also means you won't learn the skills that can make those situations easier in the future. Cliques can also keep you tied to a label you've outgrown.

Think it's hard to convince one old friend you're no longer "boy crazy" or "a gossip"? Try convincing *six*.

Groups can also stick you into another kind of rut, by branding you as a leader or follower within the group's pecking order. Which brings us to the next issue...

Leaders, Followers & Why You Should Speak Up

Have you ever argued with your best friend over a seemingly unimportant decision, like whose house to sleep over at, or whose idea to use for the Spanish Club's bake sale poster? On the surface, those discussions *aren't* really just about posters and houses—they're also about balancing the seesaw of compromise that keeps your friendship healthy.

In a fair friendship, everyone has an equal voice in making decisions.

In a healthy, happy group of friends, you'll hear the same gentle back-and-forth you hear in one-on-one friendships. But in other groups, a weird thing happens. Some people just won't speak up... even when they have something important to say! Some girls find it easier to let other people make the decisions. Others figure there's no point in speaking up when whoever's most popular will get her way anyway. Still others find it intimidating to go against an entire group. But no matter what the reason...

It's not good enough.

Think of it this way: If you stay passive, it's 100 percent guaranteed that your friends won't listen to you or respect your opinions—they won't even know what your opinions are! Scary as it may seem, you have everything to gain from taking an active role. Odds are your friends will welcome your input. If not...well, you'll know that it's time to find friends who *do* appreciate you. And when you think about it, does it really make sense to let people walk all over you because you're afraid of losing them? Heck, no. True friends don't like you only when you're a quiet "follower." So go on—speak up! Most likely your friends will show you the respect you deserve, you'll know you *really* belong...and you'll all have more fun.

You have nothing to lose—and everything to gain—by speaking your mind.

> " I feel like some of my friends don't have opinions. They don't introduce us to new stuff or come up with cool ideas for anything. They just expect us (me and my best friend) to plan everything and do everything. So we end up making the decisions."
>
> —Julie, age 13, Wash.

The Smart Girl's Approach to Cliques

By now, you may be thinking that it would be cool to bask in the support of a whole busload of friends...yet at the same time, you're not sure you want to commit to having lunch with the same folks every single day of middle school. Is there any way to balance the desire to belong to a group with the need for more freedom? Absolutely.

You can probably think of at least one girl in your school who doesn't belong to any one group, but who gets along with everyone. At lunchtime, she sits with different people on different days, or bounces from one group to another. It's true that not being a full-time member of a clique means she doesn't get invited to every group slumber party or told every juicy group secret. Still, her "open" approach to friendship offers huge advantages. She's found a way to float easily from clique to clique...without feeling tied down to any. As a result, she enjoys more friendships than almost anyone else. Want to do the same thing?

🦋 Switch on your social butterfly! 🦋

Here's how:

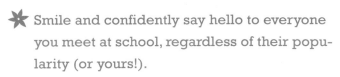

✳ Smile and confidently say hello to everyone you meet at school, regardless of their popularity (or yours!).

✳ Ask friendly questions like, "How was the final?" or "Are you doing anything cool this weekend?"

✳ Once a week or so, invite someone new over to your house for sports, games, and movies—the kinds of activities you can do even with people you don't know well.

✳ During your school lunch period, put on your best friendly smile and walk right up to a group of people you don't know well. Briefly join their conversation, then move on.

Yes, it takes a lot of courage at first, but the more you do it, the easier it'll get...until finally it becomes second nature. In the meantime, the key is to appear relaxed—even if you feel so eager to be liked that relaxation seems like a joke. If it helps, pretend you already know hundreds of people, so it's not that important what these guys think of you.

The good news is that most people you approach will be more than happy to talk to you. Why wouldn't they be? You're a friendly, fun person. And as for those few who *don't* want to chat with you unless you're a card-carrying clique member, well, you can always wave and be on your way. However, don't be afraid to go back and sit with the same group in a few weeks or months. Groups change over time, just as people do. Who knows? You just might "clique" with them better the second time around.

??QUIZ?? Is Your Group a Bad Clique?

 Still not sure how your group measures up? Take this quiz for some insight.

1. If your clique ever formed its own country, it would be:

a. A democracy...everyone with equal power.

b. A happy kingdom...sure, one of you is a little bit more popular than the others, but it's not like she tells you what to do. (Much.)

c. A state of unrest...arguments flare up daily as the battle for control marches on.

2. Bummer! You've been placed on a different after-school basketball team than your pals. When your teams face each other in the playoffs, you plan to:

a. Play your best, as always. It's only a game, so you know there will be no hard feelings!

b. Give 110 percent—proving to your friends that you've got skills is a matter of pride!

c. Hold back some of your best moves. You don't want to catch grief from your friends later if you beat them.

3. Your crew is known throughout the school for your stellar:

a. Volunteer efforts. Whether it's recycling paper or running a food drive, you're all dedicated to making the world a better place.
b. Sense of style. Your fashion choices express who you are.
c. "Investigative skills." Your friends know the status of every school crush, friendship, or relationship at all times!

4. At the local amusement park, an odd number of your friends lines up to ride the roller coaster. Which one of you has to share her seat with a stranger?

a. Whoever is last in line—it's only fair.
b. Whoever doesn't grab herself a partner fast.
c. Probably you…as usual.

5. Your mom insists you go to school in the pink polka-dot dress Aunt Hilda sent for your birthday. Your friends:

a. Totally don't care—your fashion statement, your business.
b. Make a few snarky comments at break, then let it go.
c. Insist you put on a sweater to protect the group's reputation.

more on next page!

6. You've landed an after-school dream job: modeling for a local kids store's catalog! Your friends:

a. Demand their own copies of the catalog so they can show off their "famous" friend!
b. Meet your news with stony silence. If you didn't know better, you'd say they were jealous!
c. Start a rumor that you're anorexic.

7. The new girl from another country is wearing a white shirt and *tie(!)* today. Your clique has a huddle and decides to:

a. Invite her to join your lunch table. Just because she's not wearing an A&F T-shirt doesn't mean she's uncool.
b. Give her a tour of the school, cracking jokes about her outfit along the way. Hey, it's not like she can understand you!
c. Tape a "Kick me, I'm new" sign on her back—maybe it'll encourage her to dress a little cooler tomorrow...

8. Be honest. When you've got a problem with someone in your clique, how does it get resolved?

a. You confront her right away and talk out the issue till you both feel good about it.
b. You put off confronting her and complain to someone else instead. Tension builds up until you finally explode at your friend, causing a group mega-fight.
c. It doesn't. You can't risk losing your friends, so you don't bring it up. Ever.

Add 'em up!

Mostly A's
Fabulous Friends

Your friends bring out the best in each other. You're supportive
of each other's successes and understanding of each other's
differences, not to mention kind and inclusive to those outside the
group. Count yourself lucky...your friends are totally cool!

Mostly B's
About Average

Life isn't always perfect in your little clique, but overall you're happy
to call it home...for now, at least. What can you do to make group
life better? First, make some friends outside your group so you're
not too dependent on them. Second, make the most of your time
in the group by joining in on conversations and planning your get
togethers. No matter what happens with the clique long term, you'll
be happier now.

Mostly C's
Creepy Crew

Um, remind us why you like these girls? They're snobby, they're
mean, and they love to exclude people. Worst of all, you're afraid
to be your wonderful self around them! Don't you know that group
friendship can be so much better? Check out Chapter Seven to see
what you're missing!

Chapter four

This Friendship Is *So* Over

Every ending is a new beginning.

–Proverb

When a Friendship Ends

Many lifelong friendships—even the good ones—don't survive the move to middle school. Sometimes the end is fairly painless...you just drift apart. Maybe you're no longer in the same classes, and you start making friends with the girls you see every day. Or maybe you just start to have different interests. Whatever the reason, you're both ready to move on, and the friendship just sort of fades away.

Unfortunately, it's not always that easy. Often one girl wants the friendship to continue, while the other is ready for a change. Feelings get hurt, and all kinds of drama follows. Let's look at some common ways friendships end—and the best ways to handle them.

When You're the One Moving On

You've tried, you really have. But your old BFF is getting on your nerves. You're just not into the things you used to do together, but when you try doing something new, she's bored. You're happier hanging out with other girls or even being alone, but when you try to distance yourself, she shoots you hurt looks. You feel guilty about it, but you're ready to end this friendship, even if she's not.

Remember, you've been good friends for a long time. Be kind. Take her aside and have a gentle, honest talk with her. This isn't the time to list her faults or the 10 most annoying things she's done. Just say you care about her a lot, but you feel like you want to spend more time with other friends right now. No matter how nicely you say it, she's bound to be hurt. (You would be, too.) But even if you feel mean, it's *more* unkind to string her along and let her think you're still BFFs.

> Even though it's hard, it's better to tell the truth, so she can start moving on, too.

But what if you've just realized that this friendship was never that great? What if she *hasn't* been there for you—in fact, you feel like she's consistently been mean and careless of your feelings? Tell her honestly what the problem is, such as, "I feel like you're really mean to me when other people are around." There's always the chance she'll learn something from your exit. More likely, though, she'll disagree and become defensive. Watch out—don't get caught up in a big messy fight. Attacking her won't help matters, even if you feel justified. Just make it clear you're not going to participate in some big drama war: "I don't want to fight with you. I just think it's better if we hang out with other friends from now on." Then do it.

> "She wasn't interested in making up, and finally I realized I had to just let it go. If I was the only one who cared about it, we no longer had a friendship to save."
>
> —Samantha, age 11, Mo.

When She Decides to End It

What if you're on the receiving end of the "I-don't-want-to-be-friends-anymore" speech? *Yee-ouch.* A rejection like that can be a real blow, especially if you thought everything was fine. You might even feel so shocked that you refuse to believe it's really over, that if you somehow put up a fight, you can change her mind. But if she's flat-out telling you she doesn't want to be best friends anymore, it's better just to respect her decision. Be glad she's brave enough to tell you the truth—it's not easy being in her shoes, either. So tell her you're glad she told you, and try to part ways without any unnecessary drama.

It's also possible that your BFF will decide she wants to end the friendship, but doesn't know how to tell you so. If you think she's avoiding you or you're just not sure she still wants to be friends, ask her. You may feel a little uncomfortable, but in the long run it's better to know than to keep wondering what's going on.

" My best friend and I are growing apart. We have been BFFs since we were five. She always ditches me for the popular kids who don't really even like her. I miss e-mailing her, calling her, instant messaging her, and just hanging out with her. The worst part is that she tries to embarrass me in front of boys. Please help me!"

—Letter to Ask Ali

We Were BFFs...Now She's Popular

Too often, middle-school friendships fall apart when one girl suddenly sees a chance to become "popular." Unfortunately, though, it's not the kind of popularity that comes from being well-liked and respected by everyone. (We'll talk more about the two kinds of popularity in the next two chapters.) Instead, she wants to join a crowd that gets its power from putting other people down...and part of the price of admission is pointing out just how uncool her old BFF is.

If this happens to you, you might begin to wonder, "What's wrong with me?" Remind yourself that she's the one who's changing fast; you're the same person you were last month, back when she wanted to be

No matter what, she's just a girl who's struggling to find her way...

" In sixth grade my best friend suddenly started ditching me to hang out with girls who weren't even nice to her. They were cooler than me but they also made fun of her behind her back. I tried to tell her but she said I was just jealous. She was so mean to me, I didn't even care when they dumped her."

—Reena, age 13, Fla.

your BFF. So if you were a cool, worthwhile person then, you're still cool and worthwhile now. But if your formerly sweet best friend is ditching you for girls who act like the frenemies described in Chapter Two, she's feeling so insecure right now she'll go against what she knows is right to feel important.

Yes, what she's doing stinks, and you have every right to feel hurt and angry. But try to find it in your heart to feel a little sorry for her, too. No matter what, she's just a girl who's struggling to find her way in a confusing world.

Your friend has made some lousy choices, but she might be about to learn a lesson about friendship—the hard way!

So what happens next? There are a few possibilities. Your old best friend may enjoy her status in the popular clique so much that she's willing to go on paying the price of membership. If that's the case, there's not much you can do but let her go...and move on. There's also a chance she'll come to her senses in a week (or a month, or more) and realize these girls aren't the friends she needs. At that point, she may be eager to come back to you, and it will be up to you to decide whether you're willing to forgive and start over. But don't wait around. Remember, you're still the same cool person you were before...so go find some new friends of your own.

Friendship Advice From Older Girls

"You should have more than one close friend at school, or you're really going to be lonely if that friendship ends."

—Julie, age 15, Calif.

"Understand that there's no such thing as 'stealing' friends. If your BFF gets along with someone else better, that's too bad, but people have the right to choose their friends."

—Kerry, age 14, Md.

"Don't think that it makes you bad or disloyal just because you grow apart from a good friend—it doesn't."

—Shelly, age 14, Fla.

"Don't bother trying to get a friend who has dumped you to like you again. Instead, work on making new friends who like you without you having to convince them. You'll be a lot better off!"

—Jennifer, age 16, Maine

"Remember that daily fights and drama are way more stressful than ending a friendship."

—Regina, age 16, Miss.

Top Five Reasons to Let a Friendship Go

1. **Nothing makes you want to call her.** It used to be that every tiny milestone in your life sent you running to the phone to give her an update ("I finished my homework!") Now it seems like weeks fly by before you even think about contacting her, maybe because deep down you're worried you have...

2. **Nothing to say to each other.** You used to finish each other's sentences....now when the two of you hang out, it's more like neither one of you can finish a sentence! In the awkward silences, it seems hard to believe you ever used to chat and laugh for hours, especially considering that you two now have...

3. **Nothing in common.** It's not just that you disagree about everything from pets to pop stars, it's that sometimes it feels like you're not even speaking the same language. Sadly, if the two of you were to meet today for the first time, you'd be more likely to be enemies than buds! Which is no doubt why you lately find yourself with…

4. **Nothing good to say about her.** These days you've been noticing your friend's flaws more often than her good points. You've even been tempted to talk about her behind her back to another friend—and that's a line you never would have dreamed of crossing before! All signs point to a sad truth:

5. **Nothing works like it used to in this friendship.** The two of you had something great—you clicked! Now, every time you try to say something supportive it comes out sounding wrong and makes matters worse, and every time you get together to have fun it ends in frustration.

But is it really time to back away from this friendship—or will you two weather this dry season together and come back closer than ever? Only you can decide.

Chapter Five

Stop Playing the Popularity Game!

"Unless we're happy with ourselves, popularity is meaningless."

—Camy Baker, author

The Price of Popularity

Chances are, a part of you doesn't quite believe **your mom when she tells you** "There's more to life than being popular." And you're not alone. Almost every girl fantasizes about being the coolest in her school, watched and admired by all. Treated like royalty. Adored. Envied. Crushed on. Welcomed at every cafeteria table and invited to every party.

If you ever rose to great heights of popularity, you'd probably get to experience most of these things. And some of them would feel fabulous—we're not going to deny there are perks to being known as the coolest girl in the in-crowd! Being an attention-magnet can be fun (sometimes), and you'd certainly never have to look too far for friends and admirers. But chances are, being the most popular girl at school wouldn't make you feel as good as you expect it would.

I try my best to be nice to everyone—but it is hard to sympathize with someone when you're totally jealous of her!

For example, when the whole school is abuzz with gossip about your private business, it feels just as uncomfortable as it does when you're not part of the in-crowd. Being envied isn't all it's cracked up to be, either. After all, it's really tough to feel sympathetic towards someone when you're jealous of her or feel like she has everything. The glares and behind-your-back insults don't sting any less when you're popular.

Plus, you have to deal with brand-new problems, like fake friends who only pretend to like you because they're hoping being around you will make them cooler. Constant attention? That means people watching (and judging) your every move! And good luck getting a moment free for yourself—everybody's chomping at the bit for a slice of your time. Finally, being mobbed with invitations means having to say no to some, and plenty of people won't hesitate to get mad at you or call you a snob because you didn't pick them this time. Knowing all that, do you still want to be the most popular girl at school?

Yes? That's what we thought. In fact, we're betting you want it as much as you ever did. Why? Because it's just human nature to imagine it'll (somehow) be different for you. The dream of popular perfection lives on. The sad part is that many girls would do anything to make it come true for them.

Which brings us to our next question: What are you willing to do to try to boost your popularity? Are you willing to *(gulp)* cause yourself harm? Oh, we know you'd never risk your health and safety. For example, you'd never smoke a cigarette because you were pressured to, or jump a high fence on a dare. But there are other ways to hurt yourself chasing A-list status. Have you been bruising your self-esteem and spraining your sense of self-worth by accepting less-than-respectful treatment from the popular people you call friends?

??QUIZ?? Are You a Wannabe?

When it comes to popularity, where do you draw the line? Here's a cool quiz to help you find out!

1. The popular crowd declares that pants are in and skirts are right out. Your favorite clothing item? A short black skirt. You:

a. Keep rocking that look and ignore any flack you get from the pop squad.

b. Tell your mom you just can't find that skirt and ask her to take you shopping for some pants.

c. Start phasing the skirt out—from now on, it's weekend wear only!

d. Proudly wear the skirt as a badge of rebellion against the populars.

2. The Queen of Cool invites you to her exclusive pool party this Saturday—but she makes it clear your best friend's not on the guest list.

a. Promise your BFF you'll call her to dish about the party the minute you change out of your swimsuit.

b. Tell Her Majesty that unless she invites your friend, too, you won't go anywhere near her stupid pool.

c. Say you'd really love to go but you're already busy that day…then hang with your BFF instead.

d. Tell the Queen, "She's not exactly my friend, she's just this girl who keeps following me around. Anyway, what time's the party?"

3. You just found out you weren't invited on a ski trip with the five most popular girls in class. You:

a. Don't even like to ski, so you don't give it a second thought.
b. Can't help feeling left out—you're friendly with those girls, so why weren't you included?
c. Feel panicked. You can almost feel a big red L forming on your forehead.
d. Shudder at the thought of being trapped in a cabin with those clones all weekend.

4. Think about your most popular friend. If her A-list clique suddenly kicked her to the curb, you would definitely:

a. Delete her e-mail addy pronto. Face it: Without her cool connections, who is she?
b. Like her even more now that she's not part of the Evil Popularity Machine.
c. Offer some chocolate and a sympathetic ear to vent to—popular or not, she's still your bud.
d. See a bit less of her. It's hard to admit, but maybe you are drawn to her partly for her social status.

more on next page!

5. As a brown belt in karate, you get to be an assistant teacher at your dojo. When two of your most popular classmates show up at a class for beginners, you:

a. Linger a few extra minutes with them. Maybe they'll ask you to hang out after class!
b. Ask your teacher if you can help out in a different class. Seeing those snobs every week would have ruined your favorite activity!
c. Ignore the other students and lead a private class for your two cool new friends.
d. Give them a smile and wave of recognition, then treat them just like everyone else.

6. Gossip explodes when your friend breaks up with her boyfriend. Suddenly all the popular girls who rarely talk to you are crowded around your locker, pumping for details. You:

a. Feed 'em a few choice tidbits. It's nice having the cool crowd hanging on your every word.
b. Tell those vultures it's none of their business and slam the locker door in their faces.
c. Say, "If you want to know, ask her." You don't tell your friends' secrets.
d. Spill your guts. Sure, your friend will be a bit upset (read: fuming) but it's worth it for the chance to bond with school royalty!

Give yourself the following points for each of your answers, then add them up to find your score:

SCORING
1) a. 2 b. 4 c. 3 d. 1   4) a. 4 b. 1 c. 2 d. 3
2) a. 3 b. 1 c. 2 d. 4   5) a. 3 b. 1 c. 4 d. 2
3) a. 2 b. 3 c. 4 d. 1   6) a. 3 b. 1 c. 2 d. 4

6–10 Points Don't Wannabe

You're a nonconformist at heart with a rebellious streak a mile wide. Popular? You'd rather be anything but! Go you for being proud of your different-ness! Only thing is…when you pre-judge people for being popular, you may be cutting yourself off from great friendships. Not convinced? Think of it this way: When you hate the in-crowd, you're as focused on popularity as a wannabe. Why not just like people for who they are instead?

11–15 Points Wannabe Myself

Congratulations, you're that rare middle-school girl who doesn't care too much about popularity! A true individualist, you choose your friends, clothes, and interests based on your own values—not on whatever the cool kids are doing this week. Keep being your awesome self and people will be drawn to your special brand of coolness…whether you care or not!

more on next page!

16–20 Points Wanna Maybe

Yes, popularity means a lot to you, but there are some hard lines you won't cross to raise your social status...like betraying a friend. It's okay that popularity is on your mind—just make sure you keep your priorities in order. If you surrender a piece of yourself to be popular, you'll end up feeling slimy, even if it works.

21–24 Points Wanna So Bad

You're so desperate to reach Popularity Land, you've lost yourself along the way—and you know it. Deep down, you feel empty and unsatisfied. To change course, gather all that energy you've been throwing at popularity and focus it instead on being the very best friend you can be. When you shower your friends with love and caring, it'll boomerang back to you...and then you'll have something worth far more than a space at the "cool" table.

So...BFF or Fan Girl?

Not sure the quiz got it right? **Another way to look at your friendships is to check for these ⚑ red flags. If any of them sound familiar, maybe you're giving more than you're getting back.**

It's her way or the highway.

> "I always tried to agree with my friend because she was more popular than me. If she said she liked something I'd always say, 'Me too!' One day in front of all her other friends she said, 'I really love that new song by the Purple Horseshoes.' I said, 'Oh, me too!' and everyone laughed—there was no such band! She'd just made it all up to show everyone what a follower I was."
>
> —Kate, age 13, Wash.

Come over at 7 o'clock, not 6? Absolutely, whatever she wants. Bowling instead of a movie? Sure thing...even though your heart was set on seeing that flick tonight. At some point in this friendship, you learned to bottle up your own needs. Maybe you sensed that if you didn't let her have her way, she'd lose interest in you…and there's a chance you're right. Thing is, in a true friendship, people aren't afraid to disagree or say what they want, because they know the other person will be willing to compromise.

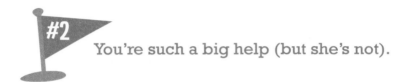

#2
You're such a big help (but she's not).

" My friend Gina was really popular, and she constantly had some kind of drama going, especially with boys. She IM-ed me about it every night...for hours. But then I got a boyfriend, and two weeks later he broke up with me. I called Gina, almost crying.' Oh, sorry,' she said.' I don't have time to talk right now.' Whatev...more like she didn't have time to listen."

         -Sherrel, age 14, Wash.

Whether it's helping her clean out her closet or listening to her complaints about another friend, you're always at your friend's service. But here's the flipside: If *you* ever needed help, you wouldn't even dream of wasting her time. After all, the few times you did start to ask a favor, she always had some excuse. In this friendship, you're the always helper, not the helpee. How fair is *that*?

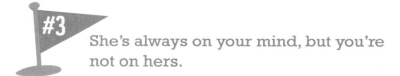

#3 She's always on your mind, but you're not on hers.

" *My friend is extremely popular, and sometimes I feel pushed aside. She has so many other friends and I've never been to her house in all the years I've known her. She rarely keeps her promises to me, and lately it feels like I'm scheduling an appointment with her whenever I want to do something. I'm starting to feel like I'm just a little fan girl in her clique.*"

—Letter to Ask Ali

The second your Spanish teacher says "partners," your head turns toward Miss Cool, but she's already high-fiving her new partner, Miss Not-You! When you call her just to chat, she's too busy to call you back. Then there's the devastated feeling in the pit of your stomach when she tells you how much fun she had at a party or at the mall, not even stopping to consider the fact that you weren't invited. It's a hard thing to come to terms with, but when Miss Cool is thinking about her friends, you're the farthest thing from her mind.

Take Back Your Self-Respect

Maybe none of this applies to you and your friendships. Maybe you're happy with your score on the "Wannabe" quiz, and none of the red flags seem familiar. If so...hey, that's great. Skip ahead to the next chapter. But if you're starting to think you might have been too focused on popularity and not focused enough on finding true friends...well, where *do* you go from here?

First, you have to admit (if only to yourself) that you haven't been the best possible friend lately. Yes, *you*! We're betting that in your quest for coolness, you've neglected some old friends who aren't super popular but have a lot to offer. If there's anyone you've snubbed that you need to apologize to, just do it. She'll probably be surprised and impressed that you can admit to your mistake.

As for that popular girl who hasn't been a great friend to you, have you honestly been a great friend to *her*? Think about it: Did you seek her friendship because you were hoping her popularity would rub off on you? If so, Miss Popular probably realizes it—and that may be one reason she doesn't feel much loyalty to *you*. Of course, that doesn't give her the right to walk all over you, and you certainly don't have to stick around for more. But if you want to make sure it doesn't happen again, you *do* have to own up to your part in this friendship drama.

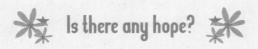 Is there any hope?

Maybe. The next time you feel pressured to do things Miss Popular's way, push back—but gently, no need to knock her over! "I'd really rather see the movie like we planned. How about if we go bowling next weekend?" is better than, "I hate bowling, and I'm sick of always doing what you want!" Be willing to compromise. You want a friendship with give *and* take, not all take or all give. If you're nervous about asking for a favor, start by mentioning a time when you stood by her: "Remember when you were totally nervous about the math test? That's how I feel about this paper. I'd really appreciate it if you'd proofread it for me." Be patient and wait for her answer. *Don't* let her off the hook with, "It's no big deal if you can't!"

If she lets you down several times in a row, it's time to stop doing this girl favors.

While it's never too late to start asking for respect, from your friend's point of view, you're changing the "rules," so it's bound to be a bumpy ride for a while. Her first response may be to get annoyed, start a fight, or make fun of you—at which point you might be tempted to apologize and go back to being her follower. Instead, hang on—you got a response from her, and that's a *good* thing, even if it feels scary. She's noticed the new, stronger you—a you who cares more about self-respect than chasing popularity. If you consistently hold your ground, she might adjust, and then your relationship could blossom into a true, *equal* friendship.

But what if she *can't* handle the confident new you? That's a very real possibility, and one you should be prepared for. If she pulls a disappearing act, you'll know for certain she wanted you as a fan girl, not a friend. Yes, that's painful, but it's a lot better to know now than to keep giving and giving to a friendship that's so one-sided. As we said in Chapter One, you deserve real, true-blue friendships...and this girl has just proven that you won't find it with her.

Chapter Six

How to Be Truly Popular

"Don't compromise yourself. You are all you've got."
—Janis Joplin, musician

Popularity...or Your Values?

If you were to make a list of the things that are most important to you in life, it would probably look something like this:

1. My family
2. My friends
3. Staying safe
4. Doing well in school
5. Being a good person

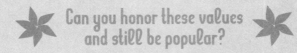

Can you honor these values and still be popular?

The answer depends on what you mean by "popular." In too many middle schools, popular means belonging to the coolest, meanest, most exclusive clique around. In that case, the answer is no. But if popular means "having a lot of friends and being well-liked and respected," then the answer is...yes, absolutely! In fact, this is *true* popularity, and you can't possibly achieve it unless you *do* stay true to the things that are important to you.

Your Best Self

Do you sometimes crack slightly mean jokes because you feel jealous or threatened? Or do you stay inside your shell, hiding the cool person you are because you're feeling shy or insecure?

If you haven't always acted like your best self, don't beat yourself up about it. Just resolve to do what you can to help the real you come out—and make more friends. And the truth is, there's a lot you *can* do. Just as it's possible to get a rep for being a gossip or a meanie, you can earn a reputation for being confident, approachable, and friendly. And those are—you guessed it—the qualities of a truly popular person!

No one acts like her best self <u>all</u> the time.

Being Confident

Projecting confidence *doesn't* mean you have a giant ego, never get scared, or won't admit to being wrong. What it *does* mean is that you set your own rules for how you dress, talk, and act based on your *own* beliefs and opinions. You don't buckle to pressure from friends or copy the popular crowd. And here's the cool part: When you have that kind of inner strength, people are naturally drawn to you. They *want* to be your friend. After all, a confident person won't be mean just to make herself look cool. She won't spill her friends' secrets, because she'd rather keep her word than be showered with attention for breaking it. A confident friend is a friend you can count on.

When you have inner strength, people are naturally drawn to you.

So what's the best way to boost your self-confidence? You've

heard the expression, "Fake it till you make it"? Try it. Act like you already have oodles of self-confidence, even if you're quaking on the inside. When you feel like freezing up, ask yourself, *What would a strong, confident girl do in this situation?* Then take a deep breath, muster up your courage, and *be* that girl. If you can manage to do this just one of every four times you feel insecure, you'll be amazed at how much your faith in yourself will grow! Before long, you won't need to fake it, because that confidence will be rock-solid real.

Of course there *is* a flip side. Just as you can build up your self-

confidence, you can also tear it down. If you often catch yourself thinking things like, *Oh, I suck at that! I just can't do it,* or if you put yourself down for doing little things wrong ("Oh, sorry! I'm so stupid!"), you'll tear your self-confidence down. Think about it: Would you say such cruel things to your best friend? Never! So remember: You should be your *own* best friend, too!

After all, if you don't treat yourself right, who will?

Being Approachable

You've seen them in the hall at school: The loud guy who swaggers and swears. The sneering girls sending out a vibe that says, "You're not cool enough to talk to us." Their message is clear: "Don't come near me!" How many potential friends are they scaring off? And they're not the only ones pushing people away. Ever see a classmate who looked like she got dressed in the dark and has a rat's nest in her hair? You probably didn't want to run right up and make friends, because her appearance told you she wasn't in control of her life. You've probably noticed that your own appearance affects how *you* interact with people, too. When you're feeling happy with the way you look, you're naturally more self-confident and outgoing.

It's true that beauty is only skin deep. But like it or not, people *do* form opinions about you based on appearances. So if you want to be approachable, it's important to take stock of what your appearance is "saying." Is your body language closed (folded arms, hunched shoulders, hands stuffed in pockets, downward gaze)...or open (head up, body relaxed, meeting people's eyes when you talk to them)? Are you scowling or smiling? Do your clothes fit right, look good on you, and reflect your style, whether that's jeans and a baseball cap or vintage dresses with boots? Remember, the goal is *not* to try to look like a fashion model, but to look *your* personal best.

Being Friendly to Everyone

You've seen it before: The so-called popular girl who is only nice to other popular people. If you're cool enough to deserve her attention, she's super friendly and sweet. If you're not, she'll ignore you or even pick on you. She might as well be saying, "You are only a worthwhile person if you are cool like me. What else is there?"

Truly **popular girls, on the other hand, are friendly to everyone.** They know that *everyone* has something to offer and *everyone* has feelings that deserve to be respected. But being friendly to everyone isn't just about what you give—it's about what you get back. If you give other people a chance by being friendly and open, they'll be much more likely to return the favor.

So what's the best way to be friendly? Be natural. There's no need to paste on a thousand-watt grin and shout compliments to everyone you meet, or hand out free cupcakes in the cafeteria as if you were running for student body president. Let small, consistent actions speak for you. Meet the eyes of a classmate when you pass her in the hall, smile, and confidently say hi. Offer a warm, "Hey, how's it goin'?" to your seatmate at the start of class. Even if this doesn't

Life is a whole lot more fun when the people around you are friends!

come naturally to you at first, the more you do it, the easier it will get...and the more casual buddies you'll be able to count at school. Sure, not everyone will respond, but many people will. And life is a whole lot more rewarding when you're surrounded by friends!

??QUIZ?? Do You Project Confidence?

Have you mastered the art of staying cool and upbeat even when you're feeling the heat? Take this quiz and find out how good you are at improvising confidence!

1. The coolest girl in your science class just got whistles, applause, *and* an A+ for her awesome report on killer whales. You're up next! You:

a. Ask if you can go tomorrow. Your throat feels really sore... suddenly.

b. Cringe and moan, "Do I haaaaave to?" and trudge to the front of the room as if you're being forced to walk the plank.

c. Force a grin and say, "Wow, *that's* going to be a tough act to follow!" Then stride to the front of the room to deliver your report on dolphins.

2. It's the first morning of theater camp and you're waiting nervously outside the building with 25 strangers (the other campers). You:

a. Stare at your watch. It's only another minute till the doors open. It's only another 50 seconds. It's only....

b. Turn to the two girls closest to you and blurt out, "I'm so nervous about taking acting classes—I never should have signed up for this!"

c. Turn to the two girls closest to you, smile, and say, "Are you guys as excited as I am?"

3. You and a friend are at the mall trying on clothes when for some reason, you start to feel shy and insecure about your body. Time to:

a. Only try on shoes. And if your friend asks you what the deal is, shrug and change the subject.

b. Constantly mutter about how "fat" and "ugly" you look in every outfit.

c. Claim your own fitting room, so you're not tempted to compare your looks with your friend's while you're feeling self-conscious.

4. Your heart sinks when you show up for Kris's birthday party and see that she's also invited Mandy—your arch-enemy since kindergarten! You:

a. Spend half the party playing Connect Four with Kris's little sister.
b. Whisper to all your best friends that you just *know* Mandy's going to say something mean and make you cry like she did that time five years ago.
c. Pretend Mandy is just another friend of Kris's—after all, that's what she is—and be as pleasant to her as you can stand to be.

5. Oh, no! When you and your friends show up at the seventh grade dance, the first thing you all see is *your crush* slow-dancing with someone else. You feel stunned and:

a. Steal away by yourself to brood about your crush's new girlfriend. (Hopefully your friends will find you and offer hugs and words of wisdom.)
b. Sigh and tell your friends it figures; you knew he was way too cute for someone like you.
c. Announce to your friends, "Yeah, it really sucks, but I'll live," and then *try* to focus on having fun on the dance floor.

6. You've been having a rough day—and to crown it all, your friends seem to be ignoring you at lunch! You:

a. Don't say a word and look depressed. If they're really your friends, they'll notice and ask what's wrong.

b. Ask them straight up, "Do you guys hate me or something? Is that why I'm getting the silent treatment?"

c. Keep making an effort to include yourself in the conversation. Considering how rotten you feel today, there's a 95 percent chance the "ignoring" is all in your imagination.

7. Oops, your hairstylist went a bit overboard this time and gave you a shorter cut than you asked for. You're having a tough time dealing with the change, so the next day at school, you:

a. Wear a baseball cap. (And the next day…and the next day…)

b. Moan to anyone who'll listen, "Omigosh, she totally butchered my hair! I want to hide in a cave till it grows out!"

c. Sport your shiniest, dangliest earrings—might as well take advantage of the fact that people can see your ears!

Add 'em up!

Mostly A's
Vanishing Violet

When your confidence goes down, you drop out of sight! The upside of shrinking away is you're unlikely to make a foolish move and embarrass yourself. The downside is you're so scared of feeling bad that you're unlikely to make any moves at all. Plus, you're asking your friends to solve the riddle of "What's Wrong With Her?" Instead of beating a hasty retreat the next time you're feeling low, take a deep breath, remove shoulders from ears, and tell yourself, "This too shall pass!" Have a little faith and hang in there. Your confidence will spring back before you know it! Not sure where to start? Read the entry for Flexible Fiona (next page)…

Mostly B's
Down-on-Yourself Debbi

When you're feeling less-than-cool, you shout it from the rooftops! The world might think you have low self-esteem, but we think you expect the worst as a way of avoiding nasty surprises…and maybe to get the people around you to reassure you that things aren't as bad as you fear. Trouble is, when you assume every scenario is the worst case, you often create bigger problems for yourself. Not to mention, your fishing for constant reassurance is a big burden to put on friends. *You're* the main person in charge of keeping you happy, so take a hint from Flexible Fiona and cross over to the sunny side of life!

Mostly C's
Flexible Fiona

You are one cool cucumber! No one feels self-assured 100 percent of the time, but you've learned to recognize your own insecure moments...and adjust to them. In tough times, you're an expert at reassuring yourself and transforming your most negative thoughts (*I'm so scared; everyone's going to hate me*) into positive ones (*I'm excited; most people are going to like me*). Good for you for being your own best friend and building up your confidence! And yeah, sometimes despite all that effort, you *still* feel insecure...but more often than not, you succeed in flipping your mood and regaining your poise. Keep up the good work and you'll be a fabulous example to your friends!

Chapter Seven

All The Fabulous Friends You Want

(And Where to Find Them)

"Friends are like stars in the night sky. The more you have, the brighter your life will be."

–Anonymous

One BFF...or Many Friends?

Let's say you and your BFF get along better than peanut butter and jelly. She gets you. You get her. Wild horses couldn't tear you apart, which is why every lunch period finds you munching sandwiches together in the school caf, and every Friday and Saturday one of you sleeps over. You finish each other's sentences...cheer on each other's successes...and on the toughest days, you have each other to lean on. Notice anything wrong with this picture of an ideal friendship? You got it! Neither one of you has anybody else!

No matter how cool she is, one person can't fulfill your every friendship need...and you can't fulfill hers. Why not? For one thing, it just doesn't make sense to count on one person to be there, always and forever. What if her family whisks her away on a three-month trip to Europe—are you going just mope till she gets back? Besides, even if she *could* be crazy-glued to your side, it's asking too much to expect your BFF to be everything and everyone you'll ever need. And clinginess won't help the friendship last—in fact, it only guarantees that sooner or later, you'll get sick of each other.

On the other hand, having a variety of friendships makes your life more interesting—and more fun! More pals means more viewpoints, more ideas, and more info to chew on...not to mention, more opportunities to learn and grow by trying new things—tasting new foods, playing new sports, new music. Best of all, a friend for every occasion every occasion

More friends, more ideas, more fun!

Studying for the math final is suddenly bearable—even fun—when you and your study buddy are making jokes and figuring it all out together. Winning the city soccer championship is more exciting when your friends on the team are hugging you and screaming, "We did it!"

Possessive BFFs

So you've decided it's time to make other friends. What if your BFF is less than thrilled—or even acting jealous? Don't worry. It's perfectly normal. On some level, she's worried you'll replace her! The best way to calm her is to tell her the truth: Her friendship means the world to you, but you think you should *both* have other friends, too. Then make plans to do something fun with her...so she knows you weren't just talkin' when you said this friendship matters to you.

When you do make a new friend, introduce her to your BFF—there's a good chance they'll hit it off, too! If they don't, however, don't push it. You don't have to share *every* friend. Odds are your BFF will soon come around to the idea that, no matter how close you are, both of you need and deserve more than one friend.

In fact, don't be surprised if *you* feel a twinge of jealousy when you hear your BFF laughing it up across the lunch table with brand-new friends of her own. If that happens, remind yourself that just because you both have new friends *doesn't* mean your own friendship has lessened in any way. Far from it! Not only will you both be happier making a variety of rewarding friendships, but you can even teach each other some of the cool new things you learn from other friends.

Fabulous Friends Are Everywhere

Friendship comes in many forms, from the casual bud you joke around with in Language Arts, to the fellow cat lover you trade kitten pics with online, to the cousin who gives golden advice. Here are just a few of the awesome friendships you want and need in your life. Collect them all!

The Pen Pal

Checking the mail or your e-mail inbox is suddenly exciting when you're looking forward to hearing all the fascinating details of your pen pal's life in Sweden, Japan, or Morocco…plus, it's so cool that she thinks your life is equally exotic! It's surprisingly easy to open up to someone through letters—and you never have to worry about her competing with you or blabbing your secrets. One day you might travel across the world to visit her in person—how cool is that?!

First step to friendship: Ask your French teacher how you can sign up to get a French pen pal, or ask your parents to help you find an international pen pal service.

The Girl Next Door

She's *there*…so nearby you can hang with zero notice. Play a quick game of handball up against the garage. Take a magazine quiz together on your homework break. Okay, so maybe your personalities don't mesh well enough to be BFFs, or share your innermost thoughts—maybe if you weren't neighbors you wouldn't even *be* friends. But you are…and it's good to spend time with people who aren't just like you.

First step to friendship: Run across the lawn and ask if she wants to bike down to the park.

The Activity Partner

He sits by you in English and gives amazing feedback on your stories. She's on your basketball team…and can teach you how to improve your layups. Whenever you share an activity with someone, it's a golden opportunity to make a friend. Why? Because whether the experience you share is rewarding, difficult, or boring, a special bond can form just from facing the same challenges together. No, not everyone in your ballet class will become your friend, but odds are excellent that *someone* will if you make an effort to connect.

First step to friendship: This is one of the few times where a little complaining is okay—in fact, it's a great low-stress way to start a conversation rolling. "Wow, I can't believe this is due tomorrow! Can you?" will get a response, and you're off and running!

The Summer Buddy

Even a boring trip can turn into an unforgettable adventure when you have a friend to share it with! Besides, when you meet someone at camp or on the beach in Hawaii, she's guaranteed to see you for who you are today, not the Girl Who Had a Most Embarrassing Moment in P.E. two years ago. Best of all, hanging with someone who doesn't know your image ("the shy girl"? "the tomboy"?) can free you to show different sides of your personality. Be sure to exchange e-mail addresses so she can become your pen pal afterward!

First step to friendship: Relax (you're on vacation!), introduce yourself...and ask if you can borrow some sunscreen!

The Guy Friend

No, of course you don't need a *boy*friend—but you do need a *guy* friend or two, cool boys who can make you laugh at their jokes or get lost in the fun of a water balloon fight or video game. Getting a guy's perspective on your problems can be refreshing, and many girls report less drama with their male BFFs than with their female pals. Just because you can't share clothes doesn't mean you can't be best friends!

First step to friendship: Humor. Guys love to joke around and even tease—so when you're first talking to a potential guy pal, just focus on keeping it light.

The Wise Woman

A bad grade. A fight with your best friend. A first crush. Who do you talk to? The wise woman. Maybe she's a little bit older than you, or maybe she's just naturally smart about people. Either way, the advice that this friend gives is priceless…and her support can help you through the toughest times.

First step to friendship: Is there an older cousin, aunt, school counselor, or coach you admire? Ask her for advice—and then be sure to thank her for taking the time to encourage you.

The Stylist

Her hair is always perfect, her clothes always look great on her… yet somehow, it's not totally annoying. That's because the stylist isn't a snob—she just happens to be savvy about style, and always willing to help her friends improve their own fashion sense. She'll help you fix up your room, cheap. She'll show you how to put together the clothes in your closet in totally new ways, or tell you which colors work best for you. Hanging out with her teaches you to notice the little things, and makes you feel more confident. Learn from her…then pay her back by teaching her something *you're* brilliant at!

First step to friendship: Get her attention with a sincere compliment: "I love the way those silver earrings frame your face!"

The Bold Chica

She's confidence in human form. This girl wouldn't hesitate to wear sparkly purple boots to school, run for class president, or stand up to a bully...and her brave example inspires *you* to be a little bolder, too. Best of all, while she encourages you to stretch your comfort zone, she never pressures you to be as daring as she is—she likes you for who you are.

First step to friendship: Next time you see her boldness in action, tell her how much you admire her courage. Follow up with an invite to do something slightly adventurous this weekend...odds are she'll be up for it!

Chapter Eight

Be the Best Friend You Can Be

"A real friend is one who walks in when the rest of the world walks out."

–Anonymous

A True Friend...Like You!

This chapter has some great tips on how to be a really good friend—including how to disagree without destroying your friendship. But first, why not take this cool quiz to find out how well you're treating your friends right now?

??QUIZ?? Are You There for Your Friends?

1. Your best friend confides in you that her older brother sometimes drives drunk...and she swears you to secrecy. You:

a. Do as she asks and keep the secret.
b. Ask your parents for advice...you value your friend's safety more than you care about her not being mad at you.
c. Tell some people at school. It's too juicy to keep to yourself!

2. You've always thought cheerleading was sort of a dumb sport, but now that your BFF's got her heart set on making the squad, you:

a. Agree not to make fun of Rah-Rahs anymore.
b. Decide to try out as well. After all, you wouldn't want her to make new friends on the squad and leave you in the dust...
c. Sit in the bleachers during her tryouts to be her cheerleader, even though it means staying at school till 5:30.

3. Busted! Your friend's parents grounded her for two weeks: No phone, no Internet, and definitely no going to the mall with you on Saturday. You:

a. Complain that it's unfair your plans got cancelled when you did nothing wrong.
b. Let her vent at lunch about how tough it is having strict parents, without pointing out that it was her fault she got in trouble.
c. Pull your five favorite books off the shelf, jot down a friendly note in each one, and pass them to her at school— she's going to need them!

4. Your friend's dad was diagnosed with a serious illness. Your main way of showing support is:

a. Constantly finding ways to help her and her family, such as babysitting her little sister or riding with your friend to the hospital.
b. Telling her, "I'm so sorry, I wish I knew how to help."
c. Hanging out with her—because honestly, she's pretty hard to be around right now.

5. Your best friend gets a D– on the math test and bursts into tears. You:

a. Tell her you're none too thrilled with your own B+. It should have been an A!
b. Give her a hug and tell her everything's going to be okay.
c. Give her a hug and tell her everything's going to be okay, then help her put together a solid plan to improve her grade.

Give yourself the following points for each of your answers, then add them up to find your score:

SCORING 1) a. 2 b. 3 c. 1   3) a. 1 b. 2 c. 3
2) a. 2 b. 2 c. 1   4) a. 3 b. 1 c. 3
5) a. 1 b. 2 c. 3

5–8 Points Give a Little!

It's great that you're in touch with your own feelings and needs, but stop and think: Your friends have needs and feelings, too, and you're too busy thinking about your own to even notice. Next time a friend reaches out to you, open your eyes and look for a way to help her out. If she's a true pal, she'll do the same for you one day. When it comes to friendship, the more you give, the more you get.

9–12 Points Give a Little More

You're a good friend, but sometimes you hold yourself back from going the extra mile to be a "wow" friend. If you've been hurt in the past or just haven't experienced a truly great friendship before, it's understandable that you're shy about giving too much. Yes, true friendship is 50-50, but that's in the long run. On any given day, one person is often giving more— and trusting that her friend will give back when it's her turn. So take a leap of faith, and from now on, give with your heart, not your calculator!

13–15 Points Giving It Your All

Wow! You're not just a good friend, you're an angel—always there for your friends when they need you, and always ready to put your creative mind to work helping them find solutions to tough situations. You give a lot and you deserve to get a lot in return…so our only question is, are your friends good enough for you? Someone like you deserves the best!

Being the Kind of Friend You'd Love to Have

You already know what makes someone a bad friend...now, what about a good one? For starters, good friends aren't (usually) guilty of poisonous behaviors. But, as we all know, there's more to being good than simply not being bad. And while every true friend brings to the table a unique blend of qualities, just about every true friend will have these same four fabulous habits:

 ## A true friend is *considerate*.

It's normal to think of yourself and your needs first—after all, you're the star of your own life. When you're with a friend, though, you choose to become costars. Her feelings and needs are just as important as your own.

A true friend is *trustworthy*.

There's more to being a rock-solid friend than avoiding huge mistakes (like blabbing your friend's secrets to the whole school). All your actions count, even little ones: being on time, remembering plans, and doing what you say you will.

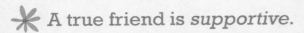

A true friend is *supportive*.

Do you support your friend by complimenting her, cheering her accomplishments, and reminding her that she's smart, brave, and fabulous? A friend is like a magic mirror—if she sees that you have faith in her, she'll believe in herself more. Choose friends you can believe in, and the rest will come naturally.

A true friend is *fun to be around*.

Are you drawn to people who smile and laugh a lot? Who like to do things? Who see the bright side of life? If so, you're not alone! That *doesn't* mean you should act fake-happy when you're genuinely upset or discouraged. But most of the time, your mood is what you make it. So put on a happy face, and see if your friends catch it, too!

Seven Ways to Handle Conflict

Arrggh...conflict. If only we could just avoid it. Some people try. They blow off steam by complaining to everyone except the person they're mad at. Or they put a lid on their feelings, pretending everything is just fine when it's not. Either way, nothing gets resolved…and eventually the situation explodes like a keg of dynamite. Then…it's bye-bye friendship. There's a better way. Here's how:

1. Deal with problems as they occur.

Don't let small wounds fester. You're hurt about something she said? Take her aside and tell her. Maybe her comment about the "weird" color of your eyes was actually a compliment: She meant they're unusual—and beautiful! Or when she said you'd never have a boyfriend, she was referring to the fact that you don't *want* a boyfriend now. Misunderstandings happen, but if you clear them up quickly, they won't blossom into major resentment.

2. Express your feelings honestly but kindly.

You're mad: She said she'd come over to help you study for the big math test, then bailed at the last minute. Or you're annoyed that she's suddenly started copying your new look. Tell her how you feel—alone—using "I feel" statements: "I felt upset that you didn't help me study after you promised you would." "I feel uncomfortable when you're always dressed exactly like me." You might feel a little dumb, but look at it this way: You deserve to be heard, and a true friend will take your feelings seriously.

If you truly feel that a friend has hurt you, you owe it to both of you to tell her so.

3. Be easy to talk to, and a good listener.

Sometimes the shoe will be on the other foot—your BFF will have a complaint about *you*. Even if your friend tells you nicely that you've hurt her feelings, you'll probably be tempted to jump in and tell her why she's wrong. Don't. Be open to what she has to say—and the possibility that you might have made a mistake. Then tell her you feel terrible about hurting her feelings.

4. Apologize when you're wrong.

You're bound to make mistakes—we all do. When you need to apologize, do so quickly—and sincerely: "I'm really sorry. That was a mean thing to say and I feel bad for saying it." Remember, real apologies don't have excuses in them. Promise that you'll try hard not to repeat your mistake, then do your best to keep your promise.

5. Learn to compromise.

In a true friendship, neither friend gets her way all the time. You can't agree about what type of cookies to make for the church bake sale? Do half chocolate chip for you, half oatmeal raisin for her. If it's an all-or-nothing situation, compromise on something else that's of equal importance to you both: You'll make her favorite chocolate-chip cookies, but you'll listen to *your* favorite tunes while you work.

6. Agree to disagree.

What if you both have strong feelings about something philosophical and important, like whether it's okay not to believe in God, or who should be president? You're not going to gain anything by trying to convert each other, and you could easily end up hopping mad! Instead, agree to disagree. The rules: No more arguing about the topic, and no making fun of each other's point of view. Just let it be. The fact that you're willing to accept each other's point of view will become yet another testament to your friendship.

7. Always fight fair.

No matter how angry you are, never stoop to name-calling or personal attacks, like, "You're such a liar!" or "You're always so rude!" Stick to criticizing her actions, not her character: "I felt that you acted rude when you ignored me." And stick to what's happening now—don't dredge up problems from three years ago unless they are truly relevant. If things get really

Never stoop to making personal attacks.

bad, ask the school counselor if you can talk in her office so she can help you sort things out.

Acts of Friendship A to Z

A great friendship takes effort. Try these ideas for making yours stronger—and more fun!

A   Have an **ADVENTURE** together—sign up for karate, get your uncle to take you fishing, or check out the new mall downtown.

B   Start a **BUSINESS** with your pals…whether it's a one-afternoon lemonade stand or a summer babysitting club, you're bound to learn a lot by being partners.

C   Always **CALL** when she's absent from school. Don't forget to ask if she needs you to bring over her homework.

D   Help her do something she's **DREADING**: Study for a math test, clean out her closet…and do it without complaining.

E   **EAT** dinner together at her house or yours. Getting to know each other's families is part of bonding with a buddy.

F FRAME your favorite photo of the two of you and proudly display it in your room. Give her a copy, too!

G Find a GAME you're equally good at and hold a BFF tournament…the winner gets to pick the next movie you watch together!

H Get her HOOKED on an exciting book or TV series—you'll have fun "gossiping" about the characters and plot twists!

I INVENT a new smoothie recipe together, and name it after yourselves!

J Make her day with a small **"JUST BECAUSE"** present, like a paperback, sparkly pencil, or bright sunflower.

K Make a KITE together, then fly it at the beach or in a windy field.

L Always LISTEN without interrupting. It may seem like a cool trick to finish someone's sentences, but it's even cooler to let her do it!

M Put together a MIX CD or playlist of cool tunes you think she'd like.

N Remember that it's okay to say **NO** sometimes when she asks for a favor…what's not okay is to say yes and not come through.

O When she tells you something about herself, **OPEN UP** about yourself, too…you'll feel closer than if you only talked about her stuff.

P Send her a silly **POSTCARD,** even if you haven't gone anywhere. Who doesn't love to get mail?

Q Ask her **QUESTIONS** about her dreams for the future, her deepest fears, and her favorite memories, so you really get to know her.

R **REMEMBER** her favorites (color, food, beverage, animal). For example, ask your parents if they'll buy her favorite soft drink when she's your guest.

S Find a **SPOT** at school to be your special meeting place: under a tree, next to the science building—you can even give it a silly codename if you like.

T **TEACH** each other how to do something. She teaches you to draw cool fashions, you teach her to make brownies…*mmm*, looks like you both win!

UNDERSTAND that she will have other friends…and you will have other friends. True friends don't crowd each other.

VOLUNTEER to work for the same cause—let your friendship inspire you to do good together!

WAIT for her after class, even if she takes extra time to talk to the teacher or pack her stuff. It feels good to know your friend thinks you're worth waiting for!

Get **EXCITED** for her! When she's scoring goals in hockey or acing her science class, cheer her on …just like you'd want her to cheer for you.

Forget **YESTERDAY**—forgive past mistakes and live in the now.

ZERO in on opportunities to be a great friend, and you *will* be one.

What's the nicest thing a friend has ever done for you?

Dallas knows I have a hard time with math, but it comes easy to her. One week she missed band practice three nights in a row to help me study for a huge algebra test. Thanks to her, I got an A!

The guitarist I wanted for my band wouldn't even audition because he didn't believe girls could rock out. So Carmen went to his house and blasted a tape of me playing the drums...and he's been in my band ever since!

" After surgery I missed a month of school, but my BFF called me every day and hung out with me when she could have gone out with other friends. She made me laugh even when I felt terrible. "

—Lauren, age 13, Ohio

" When I was cut from the soccer team, my best friend made my favorite chocolate chip cookies and a card to cheer me up. "

—Naomi, age 12, Nev.

" When I got the lead in the school play, my best friend admitted she was jealous, but she never acted that way. She even helped me learn my lines. "

—Tara, age 13, Calif.

Chapter Nine

Summing It All Up

"Life is partly what we make it, and partly what it is made by
the friends we choose."

–Tennessee Williams, author

Friendship Rules

Mean girls and poisonous friendships will be around as long as girls go to middle school—that's a guarantee. But guess what? Wonderful friendships will be around, too! Exciting opportunities are coming up, opportunities to make the best friends you've ever had. And you're ready! Just keep in mind these eight essential rules of friendship.

Rule #1

It's easy to tell good friends from bad friends by the way they make you feel. A bad friend treats you unfairly, making you feel resentful and confused, but a true friend makes you feel relaxed and comfortable with yourself. If your friends aren't treating you with the respect you deserve, you don't have to put up with it…you can find friends that will!

Rule #2

People act mean when they're unhappy with themselves. Gossiping, bullying backstabbing—these are *not* the actions of a confident, happy person. When someone insults you, remember: It's not about you. Remember, too, that some battles aren't worth fighting. And if someone is seriously bullying you, it's time to pull in your support network. Between you, your parents, your teachers, and your friends, no mean girl stands a chance.

Rule #3

The best way to make true friends is to be the kind of friend you want to find! True friends are considerate, supportive, trustworthy, and fun to be around! There are bound to be conflicts in any friendship, but you can get past the rough spots by handling them wisely.

Rule #4

You need a variety of rewarding friendships. No matter how cool she is, one person can't fulfill your every friendship need, and you can't fulfill hers. You'll both be happier if you have several friends. You'll see more points of view and learn from different people, making you even smarter.

Rule #5

A great group of friends offers you a sense of belonging...but the wrong group can box you in.

When it comes to clubs and cliques, it's best not to be completely tied to any one group! Even if you love your clique, you owe it to yourself to make friends outside the group.

Rule #6

Popularity can be wonderful to have, but it's a terrible thing to chase after. Most girls dream of being popular, but trying to push your way into the in-crowd by kissing up is bound to backfire. So if you've been letting your more popular friends push you around, it's time to take back your self-respect and find true friends.

Rule #7

True popularity is being well-known, well-liked, and well-respected...not feared.

You can be popular while staying true to yourself—in fact, being the real you is the *only* way to be truly popular. You can build a reputation for being friendly, self-assured, and approachable. It may not come naturally at first, but with practice, you *can* do it.

Rule #8

Not all friendships are meant to last a lifetime. If only one of you is interested in saving it, there's no friendship left to save. Be kind. Take the high road— avoid gossip, backstabbing, and drama, even if she doesn't. You'll be glad you did.

DISCOVERY GIRLS

Fab Girls Guide to

Sticky Situations

All the answers

Meet the Fab Girls

Getting Unstuck

Remember when you got up the courage to tell your crush you liked him...and found out he didn't like you back? Didn't you wish you knew someone who had all the answers? Well, have no fear! Not only do we know exactly how to handle your crush (what is wrong with him, anyway?), but we also know how to deal with a gazillion other sticky situations. Like when your BFF blabs your deepest secret to the entire school...or when you make a total fool of yourself onstage. We'll also tell you how to handle being cornered by a mean dog...or stranded at the mall...and much, much more! By the last page, you'll be ready to deal with anything!

Drama, Drama, Drama

Stuck between friends? Tired of your sibs? Self-conscious about your body? Crushing big time? **You're not alone.** Every month, girls write to Discovery Girls magazine to ask Ali, our advice columnist, for help with issues like these. When it comes to girls' most troublesome questions, Ali has all the answers you need. Here, she tackles your questions on everything from family to friendship to school to boys...and much, much more. No matter what you're going through, you'll find answers to your problems inside. Ali is here to help!